Preparing Your Preschooler For Reading

Preparing Your Preschooler For Reading

A Book of Games

**Brandon Sparkman
and Jane Saul**

SCHOCKEN BOOKS • NEW YORK

First published by SCHOCKEN BOOKS 1977

10 9 8 7 6 5 4   78 79 80 81

Copyright © 1977 by Schocken Books Inc.

Library of Congress Cataloging in Publication Data

Sparkman, Brandon.
  Preparing your preschooler for reading.
  Bibliography: p. 99
  Includes index.
  1. Reading (Preschool)   2. Reading readiness.
  I. Saul, Jane, joint author.   II. Title.

LB1140.5.R4S68   649'.58   77-75284

Manufactured in the United States of America

To Robert,
Drennan, AND Betsy

Contents

Visual Games
Listening Games
Determining Skill Level
Making the Games
Using the Games
Love Is Not Enough

Preface

This book is written as though it were intended for parental use only, but such is not the case. It is difficult to prepare a manuscript containing materials of this nature, yet present the material using terms and expressions which refer to, and are appropriate for, both parents and teachers; thus the parental approach.

Teachers of nursery schools, kindergartens, day care centers, Head Start centers, and other similar educational entities will find these materials unusually effective. The suggested materials when used in education centers are usually constructed by aides, volunteers, or teachers. They can be used as a vital part of the language arts program to focus on reading readiness skills. The skills covered in this publication are the critical skills which lead to reading.

When careful placement of each child is made and the materials are used regularly, as directed, extremely gratifying results will be achieved.

Parents are now realizing that they bear a great responsibility for the education of their children. More and more often parents are asking what they can do to help their children learn. Educators are just beginning to respond effectively to that question. This book is one such response.

The materials contained herein have been used in both

formal and informal settings with very positive results. Therefore, parents and teachers should find this book to be stimulating, helpful, and practical in preparing children to read.

BRANDON SPARKMAN
JANE SAUL

I.

The Parent Role

The intellectual development of a child is largely determined between the point of conception and school age. The fortunate child is the one who has the right parents—parents who pass on strong and positive hereditary factors, but just as importantly, parents who provide their child with stimulating learning experiences and with love.

The old concept that intelligence is established at birth is not valid. Intelligence, or the ability to perceive and reason, changes with each new learning experience. Parents who provide their child with many stimulating learning experiences during the preschool years will have children who are brighter and more capable of doing well in school and in daily living than they would have been had they received less attention. Fortunate children have parents who care enough to help them develop their potential.

PARENTS MAKE THE DIFFERENCE

A couple of our acquaintance have three unusually bright children. All three children have done much better in school than either parent. They show potential far beyond that which normally would have been expected of them. What made the difference? The parents. During their early years this mother loved and cared for her children. She played games with them—games she made up, games she read about, and games the children made up. She read to them, sang to them, supplied toys for their play, and she talked with them. She was available when they needed her and was ready to answer their questions and to pose new questions for them to ponder. She listened to them when they had something to say or ideas to express. She never tired of being with her children because they made living together a game. Most times together were exciting, relaxing, or otherwise enjoyable occasions. She never pressured, never pushed. She had no game plan, no structured program or schedule for teaching her children.

This mother never had a psychology course, but she is a psychologist. She had no training in child care, but she knows most of the techniques for rearing children well. She had no training in how to teach, but she is a natural teacher. We are not all such naturals at parenting, but if we care enough, we can learn to be the kind of parents children would choose if they had a choice.

Mental stimulation sufficient to assure near maximum development isn't difficult to provide. As a matter of fact it is easy and extremely rewarding. All that is needed is a little information and a few ideas to get started.

READING—AN ESSENTIAL SKILL

Let's begin with reading. Reading is an essential skill necessary for academic success and broad occupational choice. Most parents will readily tell you that the number-one goal of education should be to teach children to read well. Yet a child's success in learning to read is affected more by parents than by the school. What are you doing to help your child learn to read—to become a good reader? Are you reading to your child? Are you helping your child see how things are alike and how they are different? Can your preschooler hear minute differences in sounds? Does your child listen well, enunciate clearly, have a growing vocabulary? You can have a profound effect upon your child's readiness for formal schooling and, more specifically, upon his readiness for learning to read quickly and well upon entry into school. All of this can be accomplished in a way which will be especially pleasing to both you and your child.

LEARNING IS SEQUENCED

Much learning is sequential in nature. This concept of learning is, in a sense, like climbing a stairway. One cannot reach the second step without passing the first step. To illustrate, a child cannot learn to recognize letters before learning to distinguish between simple objects or between pictures of familiar objects. There are levels of visual skill development, and it is important to know the level your child has attained before attempting to assist in further skill development and refinement. Similiarly, a child of school age cannot learn to multiply, with understanding, until he can add with understanding. The mastery of most skills and concepts serves as a foundation for further learning. The better the foundation your child has upon entry into school, the better are his chances of academic success.

Building skills that are needed for learning to read is what this book is all about. American parents have been warned not to teach preacademic skills to their children. The basis for exercising this caution lies in the fact that few people, including teachers, have known precisely the skills that are necessary for learning to read. This void in knowledge can result in pressuring a child to learn skills which he is not prepared to learn—thus, the warning against teaching the child at home.

Recent studies and experimentation in reading readiness

clearly show the sequential nature of certain visual, auditory, and cognitive skills which lead to reading. When activities for learning these skills are arranged in order of difficulty, simple yet rather accurate ways of determining the level of skill development in each of these areas is possible.

Such is the case in Chapters IV and V. Games which teach visual skills and listening skills are arranged according to their level of difficulty, starting with the easiest games and continuing to the most difficult game in each area. When the level of skill development of a child is determined and the sequence of the games is followed unhurriedly, there is no reason or excuse for pressuring a child to learn. These games, when properly used, can give your child a decided advantage in preparing for formal schooling.

But remember that Rome wasn't built in a day. Neither will the skills which lead to reading be built quickly. It takes time and maturity for a child to move from one level of skill development to another level, so proceed slowly, gently, lovingly, and playfully.

II.

The Right Experiences

Learning to read requires the mastery of many skills and the synthesis of these skills. A child must be able to see minute likenesses and differences in the shapes of letters and words in order to read. He must associate sounds with letters and combinations of letters and detect minor variations in sounds. The sounds representing these letters and letter combinations must be further combined to complete the sounds which represent words. The child must also understand that to read, one usually proceeds from left to right and from the top of the page to the bottom.

Reading requires more than the mere calling of words. The words which are pronounced must convey meaning to the reader; otherwise the exercise of calling words is useless. This fact clearly indicates the need for vocabulary development prior to the time a child is expected to learn to read. Additionally, the concept that reading is "talk on paper" has to be acquired.

TWO-WAY COMMUNICATION

Language operates like a two-way radio. It can be sent or received. Language is sent through writing and speaking. It is received through reading and hearing. This concept of communication is acquired rather early in homes where parents read to their youngsters regularly. For those who seldom if ever see or hear their parents read, realization of this fact comes more slowly and with greater difficulty.

READ TO YOUR CHILD

Parents are the idols of their young children. Almost all preschool-age children want to be like their parents. The children of parents who read a lot (not those whose total life is consumed by reading) are likely to have a strong desire to read. This desire is greatly strengthened when parents read to their children. Listening to a parent read stimulating books and fun books can be among the most exciting, rewarding, and tender moments of one's life. One of my earliest memories is that of sitting on my father's knees while he read a "cowboy" book to me—a book which Santa had wisely delivered. It would be difficult to stress too strongly the importance of parents' reading to their children as a means of preparing them to be good readers. Many excellent books are available for purchase or in public libraries. Some of these books are listed in Appendix A.

TALK WITH YOUR CHILD

Talking with your child is even more important than reading to him. Language is first built through talking and listening. If parents don't listen when their children talk, they stifle language development. If they don't talk with them, they deny their children the opportunity to learn effective communication. Research has shown that the intellectual development of children is greatly enhanced by parents' spending time conversing with them. Conversation is the tool used to accomplish initial language skill development.

BUILDING VOCABULARY

Vocabulary is built when you help your child understand new words—to attach names to objects and ideas. Things have names, but so do intangibles. Examples are the concepts of "good" and "bad." With us, these concepts are simply taken for granted. They have meaning to us, but to a baby they are confusing and difficult. Use of other abstract words such as "and," "but," "too," and "with" are learned through talking. If a child has heard little structured conversation before entering a school program, many of these kinds of words are foreign in nature to him and will retard his normal school progress. Several abstract words are needed in initial reading so that sentences make sense. It is difficult to teach a child the meaning and use of abstract words while teaching him to read. To the child who regularly hears and uses such words, they present no problem in learning to read.

SEEING LIKENESSES AND DIFFERENCES

Learning to read requires the ability to see likenesses and differences in detail. We see largely what we are trained to see. You can help your child grow in ability to discriminate visually by pointing out how various things are alike and how they are different. For example, you can find a great deal of pleasure and satisfaction in taking walks with your child and in spending time discovering things and talking about the things which you discover together. Grass, leaves, bugs, and dogs are just a few examples. But, more important are the details of each item which you discover. Note the likenesses and differences in the leaves. See the veins, the size, the general shape, the edges, the stems, the color, the way they feel on each side, and on and on. The more minute details one is able to see, the nearer one is to being able to read.

HEARING DIFFERENCES IN SOUNDS

Likewise, the ability to hear differences in closely related sounds is critical to reading. Phonetic skills are more easily developed in children who have had numerous experiences in sound perception. To help your child build listening skills, give him lots of experiences in hearing long sounds and short sounds. Much practice can be gained through playing games of naming all of the sounds one hears. During the preschool years most children can refine their listening skills to a point where the phonetic approach to reading is an easy transition. You can play a major role in making sure that your child has the listening skills which prepare him to read.

BUILDING CONCEPTS

Concepts are built through experiences and practice. Seeing likenesses and differences is a visual skill, and hearing likenesses and differences is an auditory skill. But the ability to classify the things one sees and hears into categories is a cognitive or conceptual skill. All leaves are different, yet when one is able to discern the details of leaves, he finds enough similar characteristics to classify them into one general category of "leaves." It takes much more than visual skills to ascertain that a St. Bernard and a poodle both belong to the canine family. These are concepts which are learned through experience. The ability to classify or categorize is a reasoning skill—a skill requiring logic.

USING LOGIC TO CLASSIFY

Being able to reach a logical conclusion with the information at hand is an important skill in reading. This skill can be enhanced in children through their observing things and discussing their observations with more mature people.

The ability to classify also assists in observation because it brings order to that which one observes. A system of classification serves as a basis for comparison. A certain kind of dog might resemble a breed of cats more than another breed of dogs, but the bark clearly distinguishes it from the cat family. Classification aids in remembering. When one can make sense out of that which is observed, it can be remembered more easily than a mass of unrelated or confused perceptions.

Certain classifications fall into a category called sequence. Examples are the parts of the day and the seasons of the year. We get up in the morning, work (or play) during the day, and sleep at night. Summer comes and is followed by autumn, then winter, then spring. We plant seeds and the plants grow, then die.

The concept of sequence is important in learning to read. Letters convey meaning if placed in certain sequence (dog) but an entirely different meaning if in another sequence (God), or no meaning at all if in another sequence (odg). Likewise, words convey meaning only when properly sequenced. Children must understand this concept of sequence before they can read with any degree of comprehension. There are many ways you can help your child to grasp this concept.

PUTTING IT ALL TOGETHER

As a child develops the ability to hear and to see likenesses and differences, to learn new and more complex words and attach meaning to each word, and to categorize information and ideas, he is building a foundation for more advanced learning and for learning at a more rapid rate. In other words, he is becoming more capable of learning or is becoming more intelligent.

PLEASE DON'T PUSH

A warning is important at this point. Parents who set up a formal learning program and push their child to learn more than the child is ready and eager to learn are making a grievous error.

Learning Through Games

Learning should be fun. If learning occurs through relaxed, gamelike activities children will approach learning in an eager and positive way. If it is forced upon them or is unpleasant they will dislike learning-type situations. The idea is to help your child learn in a way that will cause him to want to learn more. Situations in which failure or defeat is imminent should be avoided on most occasions. This statement does not mean that your child must be successful in every activity attempted. It merely means that success should be experienced much more often than failure so that he will acquire an enthusiasm for learning.

LEARNING TO SEE

Chapter IV contains games which teach children to see likenesses and differences. The first games are easy but succeeding games become increasingly difficult. Some of these games involve more than sight. Some games teach concepts. An example is the matching of lowercase letters and capital letters. The capital "A" and the lowercase "a" have little or no resemblance, yet both have the same name and represent the same sounds. These concept games are included in the visual games because they involve sight and also because they fit well in the sequence of visual games. The ultimate purpose of these games is letter and word recognition.

CRITICAL LISTENING

The games found in Chapter V are listening games. They teach children to hear likenesses and differences in sounds. The lower level games help children to distinguish between loud and soft sounds, long and short sounds, and high and low sounds. As the games progress, they require more refinement in listening skills. If the sequence of games is followed, eventually the child will be exposed to rhyming sounds and letter sounds as well as beginning sounds of words. Once the games in Chapters IV and V are mastered, it is likely that your child will be reading or will be ready for formal reading instruction.

MATURITY MAKES A DIFFERENCE

A further word of caution. Mastery of the skills which lead to reading requires years of experience and maturity. When handled properly, most children will find a great deal of enjoyment in playing the visual and the listening games. If the games are played too often or for excessive periods of a child's time, he will tire and lose interest. If the games are too difficult, he will become discouraged. If they are too easy, he will become bored. Let your child set the pace. You should always end the games while your child still wants to play, thus you sustain his interest.

VISUAL GAMES

The visual games and conceptual games contained in Chapter IV are numbered 1 through 84. Twenty-one of the

games are "placement games." They are preceded by asterisks
(*) and are sequenced according to level of difficulty.

Game number 1 is most appropriate for children ranging
in age from two to three years, whereas game number 84
would most often be appropriate for children from five to
seven years of age. All children must be able to do the lower
level games before they can master those of a higher level, but
the age at which any given game can be mastered varies
greatly with different children.

LISTENING GAMES

The listening games in Chapter V are numbered 1
through 56 and, as in the visual games chapter, the placement
games are sequenced according to level of difficulty. These
placement games are also preceded by asterisks (*).

You should use only placement games until you find your
child's beginning level. Once this level is determined, you
should use both visual and listening games alternately. The
preceding statement does not mean that your child should be
exposed to only one visual game before playing a listening
game. But it does mean that visual games should be in-
terspersed regularly with listening games and vice versa.

Many records are on the market which can be used effectively in developing listening skills. Some of these records are
listed in Appendix B.

DETERMINING SKILL LEVEL

You should read Chapters IV and V hurriedly with an
overview of the games in mind. Then you should study the
placement games carefully. In this way you will be able to
grasp the sequential nature of the games and the skills which

they are designed to teach. You will also get a feel for where your child will be able to begin in both the visual and the listening games.

In order for your child to be successful in playing these games, you will need to determine his or her skill development level. This determination can be made by estimating which of the games he can successfully play.

First note the games in which the numbers are preceded by an asterisk. These placement games are used to help locate the starting point for your child. Let's suppose that you decide that your child can successfully complete game number 16, but that game number 20 would be too difficult. You and your child should then work together in making game number 16. Each can do certain tasks such as cutting, drawing, and pasting. The preparation of the games can be as much fun as playing the games. This game preparation can be a valuable learning experience as well. Searching for pictures, cutting, pasting, and similiar activities require visual skills; therefore, practice in visual skill development is afforded as well as exercise and refinement in eye-hand coordination and in small muscle development. However, the maturity level should be considered in deciding which game preparation activities your child should be given. For example a child whose small muscle development is inadequate to handle scissors should not be assigned the task of detailed cutting. Caution should be exercised in permitting young children to use dangerous tools such as pointed scissors, which may be the only ones available in the home. Yet, even the very young child can help collect items and pictures for use in playing games. Parental judgment must be exercised in assigning roles to children.

Once the game is made, an appropriate time can be found for trying it out. If your child can complete the game, you should then prepare the next higher level placement game (one preceded by an asterisk). If this game is too difficult for your child to complete, then the game previously attempted and completed is the correct starting level for him.

If the first game attempted (in this example game number 16) was too difficult, then you should make the next lower level placement game for use with your child. You should continue to try these placement games until you find the one which your child *cannot* complete that is preceded by the placement game which he *can* successfully complete. The game which he can complete is his starting level.

MAKING THE GAMES

You and your child can now begin making the games which follow the starting level game. Each placement game is preceded by three other games of that series. These games are designed to help develop the skill measured by the placement game. They are sequenced within their own group, the first usually being the easiest and the fourth the most difficult.

After determining the starting points in both the visual and listening areas, you can proceed by making the games which follow as they are needed. The placement games from this point on should be used in the same manner as all of the other games. The games can be made when you want to spend some time with your child doing something that is fun and constructive. As a matter of fact, game making can become a game—a fun kind of time when parent and child talk and laugh and learn together. Then the games can be played with a much higher level of enthusiasm and excitement for both.

The visual games and the listening games are each numbered sequentially. Illustrations appear where needed. Materials necessary for playing the games are listed, and in those cases where games have to be constructed, the directions are given for making them. And finally, the procedures are given for playing the games.

Some games are designed to be placed on 3″ x 5″ cards. They can be made from many different materials such as cardboard, typing paper, scratch pads, or even paper sacks. If you wish the convenience of having your cards already cut to size, a package of 3″ x 5″ unruled index cards is an excellent choice.

You might like to store the games for later use. Plain envelopes will be helpful storage units and can be labeled on the front with the game numbers.

USING THE GAMES

Don't rush your child or push to obtain mastery of successive games. It takes maturity as well as practice to master visual, conceptual, and auditory skills. Don't take learning too seriously or you will "turn off" your child to learning.

A child develops in many areas and in many ways simultaneously. While he is refining his visual skills, he is also developing listening skills, speaking skills, motor skills, and social skills. Give your child time, and give attention to his total development.

LOVE IS NOT ENOUGH

These games, when used properly, should assist your child greatly in developing the skills necessary for learning to read. But we hope that the activities and interaction will do more than prepare your child to read. The use of these games should bring about a much closer relationship between your child and you. Also, you should acquire a better understanding of the learning process and perceive how you can assist your child to learn throughout his or her school years.

A healthy parental concern for children and a positive

attitude toward schools and learning are directly related to a child's academic achievement. A warm, caring atmosphere is conducive to learning. Learning without love is a tragedy, but love alone is not enough to assure your child of personal success. Good luck!

IV.

Visual Games

1. Materials needed:
    2 matching socks
    2 matching shoes
    2 matching gloves or mittens
   Procedure:
   Place all objects unmatched on a table. Ask your child to place together those that are alike. Give help if necessary.

2. Materials needed:
    2 identical envelopes
    2 identical cups
    2 identical saucers
   Procedure:
   Place all objects unmatched on a table. Ask your child to place together each pair of objects that are exactly alike.

3. Materials needed:
    1 egg carton
    3 matching pairs of small items, such as buttons, nails, pennies, marbles, dried beans, etc.

   Directions for making:

Cut an egg carton in half crosswise, leaving six compartments as shown in the illustration.

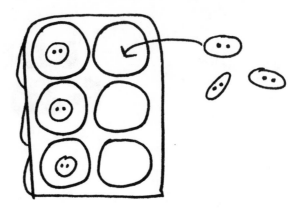

Procedure:

Place one item of each pair in a column down one side of the egg carton. Place the three matching items on a table before your child. Ask your child to place the three items in the empty compartments of the egg carton, each one beside its matching item.

*4. Materials needed:
2 identical spoons
2 identical forks
2 identical table knives
2 identical large nails
2 identical safety pins
Procedure:
Place all items unmatched on a table. Ask your child to show you which objects look exactly alike.

5. Procedure:
With your child, look around the room and find things that are exactly alike. You might see windows, door

knobs, handles on cabinets, and so forth. Discuss how they look alike.

6. Materials needed:
   2 identical plates
   2 identical bowls
   1 saucer
   Procedure:
   Place all items unmatched on a table. Ask your child to place together the ones that are exactly alike. Which one is different?

7. Materials needed:
   2 identical envelopes
   2 pennies
   2 drinking straws
   2 forks
   1 jar top
   1 spoon
   Procedure:
   Place all objects unmatched on a table. Ask your child to place together the objects that are exactly alike.

   2 red crayons
   2 identical paper clips
   1 spoon
   1 empty bottle

*8. Materials needed:
   Procedure:
   Place all items unmatched on a table. Ask your child which ones look alike. Help place together in pairs those that look exactly alike.

9. Procedure:
   Look at the different kinds of lights in your home. Help

1 sponge
1 thread spool
Procedure:
Place all items unmatched on a table. Ask your child to place together the items that are most alike.

17. Procedure:
While at the grocery, have your child close his or her eyes as you choose an item to buy. Then let your child look at the label on the chosen item and show you where others like it are located on the shelf.

18. Materials needed:
3 comic strip pictures, 2 identical and 1 different
Directions for making:
Borrow a newspaper from a neighbor so that you have two identical comic strip sections. Cut one individual square (one picture) from one of the comic strips in one paper. Cut the same matching picture from the other paper. Also cut one additional picture from the same comic strip of one paper. You now have two pictures that match and one that is different.
Procedure:
Place the three pictures on a table. Ask your child to show you which ones are exactly alike.

19. Materials needed:
2 picture bingo playing cards
12 matching picture cards
Directions for making:
To make picture bingo playing cards score two sheets of 8½" x 11" paper into six equal sections, each approximately 3½" x 4". Using two identical magazines or catalogs cut twelve pairs of identical pictures. Paste a different picture in each section on each card. Paste the

Cut 2 playing
cards

remaining twelve matching pictures on individual 3″ x 5″ cards.

Procedure:

You can play this game with your child. Place the small cards face down in a box. Each player takes turns drawing one card at a time from the box. If he has the matching picture on his playing card, he places it on top of the picture. (Due to the size of the matching cards they will not exactly fit on the playing card. You may cut them down to size or simply let them be placed over the edge.) If he does not have a matching picture, he returns the card to the box. The object of the game is to try and match all the pictures on the card.

*20. Materials needed:
9 identical picture pairs

Directions for making:
From two identical catalogs or magazines cut two identical pictures each of the following items; dress, truck, wagon, dog, flower, hat, bed, shoe, chair. Paste each picture on a 3" x 5" card.

Procedure:
Place one set of nine different picture cards on a table.
Give your child the second set, one picture at a time,
and ask your child to show you the matching picture.

21. Materials needed:
    1 egg carton
    2 yellow buttons
    2 red buttons
    2 blue buttons
    2 green buttons

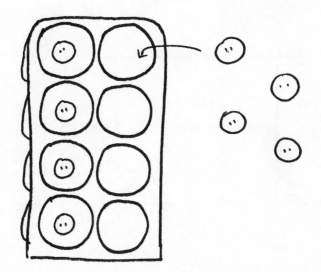

Directions for making:
Cut egg carton so that eight compartments are left as
shown in illustration.
Procedure:
Place one button of each color in a column down one
side of the egg carton. Give your child the other four

buttons and ask that each be placed in the compart-
ment beside the button of the same color.

22. Materials needed:
    Several scraps of red material, yellow material, green
    material, and blue material.
    Procedure:
    Place all scraps of material on a table. Ask your child
    to group all of the red pieces together, then all of the
    yellow, the blue, and the green.

23. Materials needed:
    1 four-color card
    4 individual-color cards

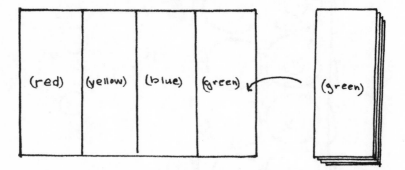

Directions for making:
    Score one 3″ x 5″ card into four sections as shown. Color
    one section red, one yellow, one blue, and one green.
    Repeat this procedure with a second card, cutting on
    the scored lines this time to make four matching color
    rectangles.
    Procedure:
    Place the 3″ x 5″ card on a table. Give the individual-

color cards to your child, one at a time, and ask that
they be placed on top of their matching color.

*24. Materials needed:
      8 colored circles

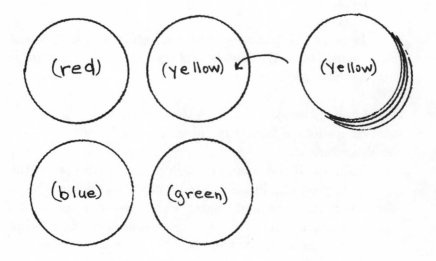

Directions for making:
   Cut eight circles 4″ across. (Find a jar top approximately this size and trace around it.) Color two red,
   two yellow, two blue, and two green.
Procedure:
   Place all colored circles unmatched on a table. Ask
   your child to place together those that are the same
   color.

25. Materials needed:
     Pictures of 4 items that can be found in your home,
     such as a chair, a table, a lamp, a rug.
     Procedure:
     Give your child one picture at a time. Ask your child to

find in your home an actual object similar to the one in the picture.

26. Materials needed:

Magazine pictures of items you might see near your home such as a tree, a house, a stop sign, a street, and so on.

Procedure:

Look at the pictures with your child and talk about them. Then take a walk and try to find objects similar to those pictured.

27. Materials needed:

Snapshots of family members and/or friends

Procedure:

Talk about the people in each picture with your child. Help your child make a group of all the pictures he or she is in. Then ones might be grouped that you are in, continuing this process by grouping pictures of other family members or friends.

*28. Materials needed:

4 pairs similar pictures

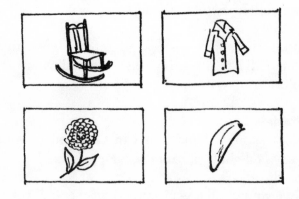

Directions for making:

From magazines cut two pictures of flowers, two of fruits, two coats, and two chairs. Paste each picture to separate 3" x 5" cards.

Procedure:

Place one picture from each pair on a table. Give the other four pictures to your child one at a time and ask that each be matched with a similar picture on the table.

29. Materials needed:

4 color cards

Directions for making:

Let your child color one 3" x 5" index card red, one yellow, one blue, and one green.

Procedure:

As your child colors the index cards talk with him about each color. Then let your child choose a favorite book and look through it to find colored pictures of each color.

30. Procedure:

Help your child think of things that are red such as an apple, fire truck, or stop sign. Continue with things that are yellow, blue, and green. Ask your child to color a picture to illustrate an item of each color. After the illustrations are finished the color cards from game 29 might be matched to the colored pictures.

31. Materials needed:
    8 colored cutouts

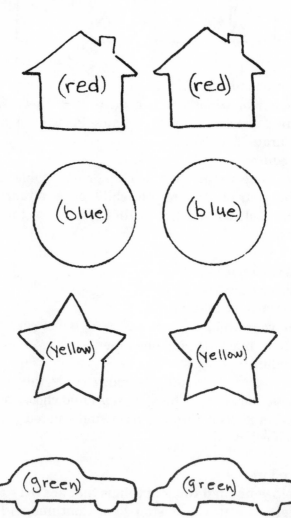

Directions for making:

Using eight 3″ x 5″ cards, draw outlines similar to those above, one per card. Color as indicated. Your child might participate in making this activity and also add other details such as windows, doors, designs, and so forth.

Procedure:

Let your child match each pair of cutouts by color.

*32. Materials needed:

8 color pictures

Directions for making:

Cut eight colored pictures from a magazine or catalog—two red, two yellow, two blue, and two green. Glue each picture to a separate 3″ x 5″ card.

Procedure:

Place all cards randomly on a table. Ask your child to match each picture to a picture of the same color.

33. Materials needed:

1 magazine

Procedure:

Play a "find it" game with your child. Let your child go first, choosing a pictured item such as a car or chair. You then try to find a picture of a similar item elsewhere in the magazine. If one cannot be located, have your child choose again. When you can find a similar picture, it is your turn to choose an item for your child to match. Continue taking turns as long as your child is interested.

34. Materials needed:

1 catalog

Cut out pictures of the following items: a ring, pair of shoes, a belt, a dress, and a sweater.

Five 8½″ x 11″ sheets of paper

Procedure:

Show the pictures to your child one at a time. Help your child look through the catalog to find a picture of a similar item. Your child may cut out the pictures similar to yours and then glue each pair onto an 8½″ x 11″ sheet of paper.

35. Materials needed:

3 pairs similar pictures

Directions for making:

Cut three pairs of similar pictures from a magazine or

catalog. For example, you might cut pictures of two beds, two lamps, two windows.

Procedure:

Place all six pictures unmatched on a table. Ask your child to place together those that look most alike.

*36. Materials needed:

3 picture cards of hats
3 picture cards of boats
3 picture cards of fish

Directions for making:

On 3″ x 5″ cards draw the pictures shown above or find similar pictures in magazines or catalogs to cut and paste onto the cards.

Procedure:

Place all nine cards unmatched on a table. Ask your child to group them into three groups of similar pictures.

37. Materials needed:
    4 pairs material squares

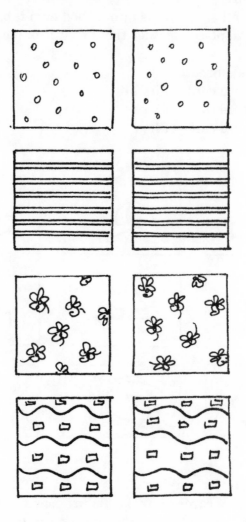

Directions for making:
  From scraps of material cut 2″ x 2″ squares so that you
  have one pair from each of four designs.
Procedure:

Place all squares of materials on a table. Let your child match each pair by color and design.

38. Materials needed:
     8 kite cutouts

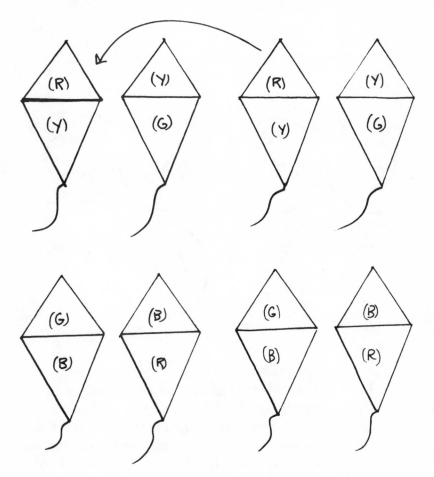

Directions for making:
   From index cards cut eight kite shapes. Color as above using this color code: R—red, Y—yellow, B—blue,

G—green. Glue on short pieces of string as tails.

Procedure:

Place one kite from each pair of color combinations on the table. Give your child each of the other four kites one at a time and ask that they be placed next to the ones they match.

39. Materials needed:

4 pairs of circle designs

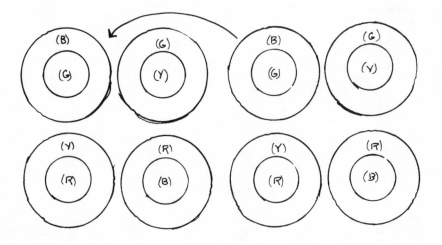

Directions for making:

From index cards cut eight circles each 3″ across. Draw a smaller circle inside each large circle as shown in the illustration. Jar tops can be used to trace around. Color the middle and outer parts of each circle according to this code and the illustration above: R—red, Y—yellow, B—blue, G—green.

Procedure:

Place one two-color circle from each pair on a table. Give the four other circles to your child and ask that they be matched with the ones on the table.

*40. Materials needed:
    8 colored design rectangles

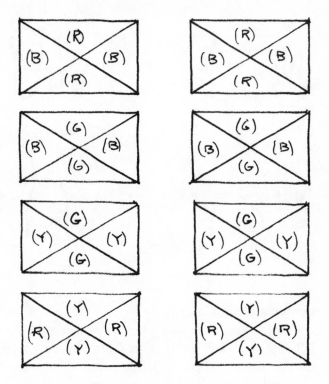

Directions for making:
    Draw from corner to corner across eight 3″ x 5″ cards as
    shown above. Color each card with two colors accord-
    ing to the code given: R—red, Y—yellow, B—blue,
    G—green, so that you have four matching pairs of
    color designs.
Procedure:
    Place one colored design card from each pair on a table.
    Ask your child to match the four other cards to those
    on the table.

41. Materials needed:
    4 hand cutouts
    4 foot cutouts

Directions for making:
    On large paper or a paper bag draw around your child's left foot and left hand. Cut from the paper two left-hand cutouts and two left-foot cutouts. Repeat this procedure drawing around *your* left hand and left foot and cutting two shapes of each.
Procedure:
    Lay all cutouts unmatched on a table and let your child place together each pair that is exactly alike.

42. Materials needed:
    5 picture puzzle cards
Directions for making:
    On each of five 3″ x 5″ cards draw or cut and glue a different picture. Cut each card differently into two parts puzzle fashion. See sample puzzles above.

Procedure:
  Place all ten puzzle parts unmatched on a table. Ask
  your child to put the pieces back together to make pictures.

43. Materials needed:
  3 pairs shape cutouts
  Directions for making:

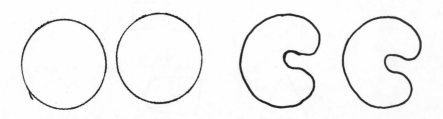

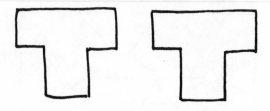

From 3″ x 5″ cards cut two each of the shapes shown as large as the cards permit.

Procedure:

Place all cutouts unmatched on a table. Ask your child to place together each pair that is exactly alike.

*44. Materials needed:
    4 shape cards
    4 shape cutouts

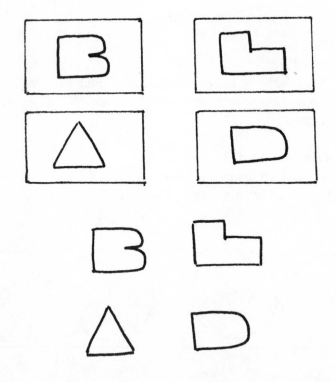

Directions for making:

On four 3″ x 5″ cards draw and cut out one each of the four shapes above. Lay each shape on another 3″ x 5″ card and trace around it to make four shape cards.

Procedure:

Place the four cards on a table. Ask your child to place the shape cutouts on top of each card that they match.

45. Procedure:

While driving, help your child locate signs such as a stop sign, yield sign, curve ahead, speed limit, or railroad crossing. After returning home, draw each of these signs on a piece of paper, and discuss again what each one means. The next time you are out driving, let your child locate each design that you have drawn on the paper.

46. Materials needed:

3 pairs of design cards

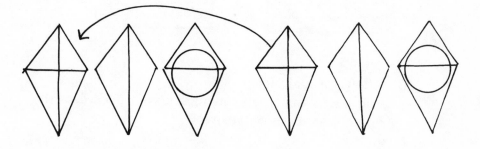

Directions for making:

Draw and cut from 3″ x 5″ index cards two shapes of each design as shown above so that you have three pairs of matching designs. The designs may be drawn with a crayon or magic marker, but the same color should be used on all the designs.

Prodecure:
Place all circles unmatched on a table. Ask your child
to place together the circles that look exactly like.

47. Materials needed:
3 pairs of line designs

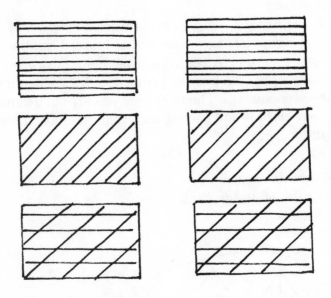

Directions for making:
Using one crayon or felt pen mark six 3″ x 5″ cards with
the line designs shown above.
Prodecure:
Place all cards unmatched on a table. Ask your child to
place together those that are exactly alike.

*48. Materials needed:
3 pairs of circle designs
Directions for making:

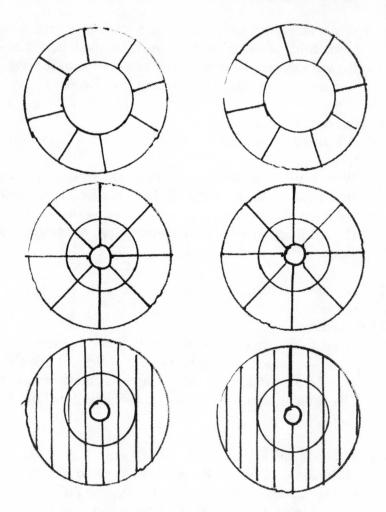

From 3″ x 5″ cards cut six circles 3″ across. Using one
crayon or felt pen copy the designs above onto the circles.
Procedure:
   Place all circles unmatched on a table. Ask you child to
   place together the circles that look exactly alike.

49. Procedure:

While stopping at an intersection during a drive with your child, ask which cars are going to the left, motioning with your hand to the left. Then motion to the right and ask which cars are traveling this direction.

50. Materials needed:
    A catalog
    Procedure:
    With your child, look at a section that pictures people in a catalog, such as the clothing section. Help your child see which people are pictured facing the middle of the catalog and which are facing outward toward the sides.

51. Materials needed:
    4 spoons
    Procedure:
    On a table lay two spoons facing opposite directions. Give the other two spoons to your child and ask that they be placed directly below yours so that they face in the same direction as each of those you placed on the table.

*52. Materials needed:
    3 car cutouts, two facing same way, one different
    3 bus cutouts, two facing same way, one different
    3 airplane cutouts, two facing same way, one different

Directions for making:

From 3″ x 5″ cards cut one cutout of a car, one of a bus, and one of an airplane. Make them as large as you can on each card. Using these as a pattern, trace around and cut out two more cars, two buses, and two airplanes, facing in the directions shown in the illustration. Your child might like to add windows, doors, or other details.

Procedure:

On the left of a table place in a column one car, one bus, and one airplane, each facing to the right. Leave a space underneath each. Place the other cutouts in two columns to the right as shown in the illustration. Ask your child to choose the cutouts in the second and third columns that are going the same way as those in the first column and to place them underneath the correct items in the first column.

53. Materials needed:

Animal cookie cutters

Pencil and paper

Procedure:

On paper trace around animal cookie cutters. Let your child then place the cookie cutters directly on top of the silhouettes.

54. Materials needed:

6 directional picture cards

6 directional cutouts

Directions for making:

On 3″ x 5″ cards cut out as large as possible one key,

one turkey, and one teapot. Reverse the cutout, trace around it, and cut a second silhouette facing the opposite direction. This makes six cutouts to match. Trace

around each silhouette on a 3″ x 5″ card to make six
directional picture cards.

Procedure:

Place directional picture cards on a table as shown in
illustration. Give the six matching cutouts to your
child and ask that they be placed on top of the directional picture and that they match.

55. Materials needed:

9 directional picture cards

(Pictures drawn on)   (Pictures glued on)

Directions for making:

From 3″ x 5″ cards cut one silhouette of a house, one of
a fish, and one of a bird as shown in the illustration.
On two 3″ x 5″ cards, first trace around the house on
one, turn the house cutout over and trace around it on
the second card. Then glue the original cutout to a

third 3″ x 5″ card. Add any details with pencil or crayon. Do the same with the fish and bird cutouts.

Procedure:

Place the drawn-on silhouette cards to the left of a table in two columns as shown in the illustration. Place the matching glued-on cutout card to the right of the columns. Ask your child to place the cards on the right with the card on the left that matches it exactly.

*56. Materials needed:

2 sets of directional picture cards

Directions for making:

On six 3″ x 5″ cards draw two identical turkeys, two identical teapots, two identical keys. On six more 3″ x 5″ cards draw the same items with reversed direction (mirror images). These twelve cards can be divided into two sets each containing a pair of turkeys, a pair of teapots, and a pair of keys facing opposite directions.

Procedure:

Place one set of pictures on a table as shown in either (left or right) side of the illustration. Give the other set of pictures to your child, one at a time, and ask that they be placed with the picture that they match.

57. Materials needed:
Pencil or crayon
Paper

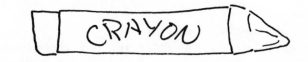

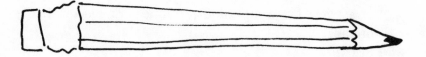

Procedure:
Draw very large capital letters, one per page on sheets of paper. Help your child name the letters. By tracing each letter with a finger, your child can learn how each letter is formed.

58. Materials needed:
A set of capital letters to feel

Directions for making:
Make a set of capital letters to feel on 3″ x 5″ cards. The letters can be formed from such materials as pipe cleaners, drinking straws, heavy cord, etc., glued onto the cards.
Procedure:
Use the letter cards with your child a few at a time, to help him or her learn how each letter is formed by feeling it, and to help begin learning the letter names.

59. Materials needed:
A set of large capital letters (can use those from game 57)
Directions:
Draw very large capital letters, one per page, on sheets of paper.
Procedure:
Begin with the letter A and show it to your child. Help

your child name the letter and then see how many different places in your home you can find this letter. If your child can do this readily, add other letters one at a time as long as he or she shows an interest.

*60. Materials needed:
2 sets of capital letter cards

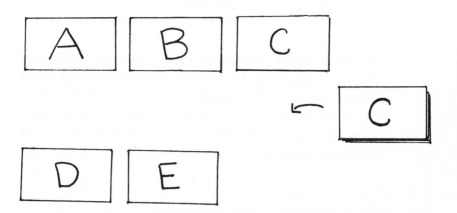

Directions for making:
On a set of fifty-two 3″ x 5″ cards, make two sets of capital letters, one letter per card, writing the letters as large as the cards allow.

Procedure:
Place five or six letter cards at a time on a table. Give the matching letter cards to your child and ask that they be matched with the letters on the table.

61. Materials needed:
A box top (such as shoe box), or cake or cookie pan
Some dry ingredients such as sand, corn meal, rice, etc.

Procedure:
Pour dry ingredients about ½-inch deep into a box top or pan. With your fingers write as large as you can one

Place five or six letter cards from one set on a table. Give the matching letter cards from the second set to your child and ask that they be matched to the letters on the table.

65. Materials needed:
    The following letters to "feel": M, W, u, n, m, w, l, i, I, L, b, d, p, q

Directions for making:
   Cover a sheet of cardboard with sandpaper, terrycloth, or any textured material. Cut the letters listed above from the covered cardboard. If you draw the letters on the back of the cardboard for a cutting line, be sure to reverse letters (mirror image) in order for the textured surface to be on top when cut out.
Procedure:
   Let your child practice feeling each letter. You can offer help by pointing out how the letters look alike

and how they look different. For example, u and n are exactly alike except one is upside down to the other; b and d look alike except they face in different directions. Help your child name the letters as you work with them.

66. Materials needed:

Block letter cards for the following letters: M, W, u, n, m, w, l, i, I, L, b, d, p, q

Cutout letters for matching

Directions for making:

From 3″ x 5″ cards cut out one block letter for each letter listed above. Place each letter on another indi-

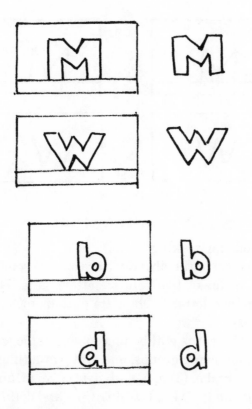

vidual index card and trace around it. Draw a line under each letter as shown. You now have fourteen block letter cards and fourteen cutouts for matching.

Procedure:

Place the following four groups of letter cards on a table, one group at a time: M and W; u, n, m, and w; l, i, I, and L; b, d, p, and q. With each group give the corresponding letter cutouts to your child and ask that they be placed on top of the correct cards.

67. Materials needed:

2 sets of letter cards for the following letters: M, W, u, n, m, w, l, i, I, L, b, d, p, and q

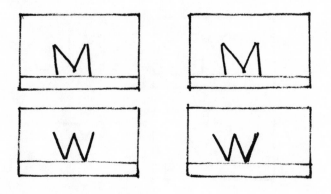

Directions for making:

Write each of the above letters on two separate 3″ x 5″ cards to make two sets of letter cards. Draw a line under each letter to show its placement.

Procedure:

The letter cards will be placed on a table for matching in the following groups, one group at a time: (1) M and W; (2) u and n; (3) u, n, and m; (4) u, n, m, and w; (5) l, i; (6) l, i, and I; (7) l, i, I, and L; (8) b and d; (9) b, d, and p;

(10) b, d, p, and q. As each group is placed on a table give your child the corresponding letter cards from the second set and ask that the letters that look exactly alike be placed together.

*68. Materials needed:

2 sets of letter cards for the following letters: M, W, u, n, m, w, l, i, I, L, b, d, p, q (can use those in game 67)

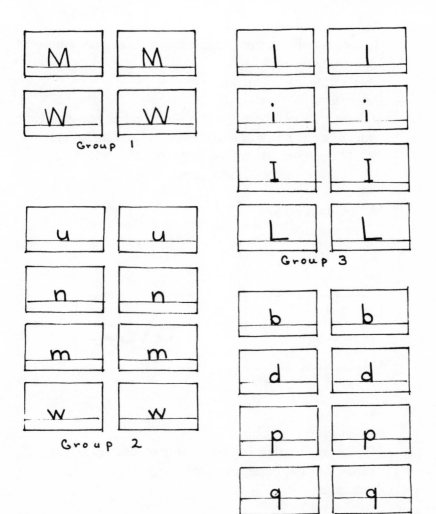

Directions for making:
Write each of the above letters on two separate 3″ x 5″ cards to make two sets of letter cards. Draw a line under each letter to show its placement.

Procedure:
Place the letter cards from one set on a table, one group at a time. Give the corresponding letter cards from the second set to your child and ask that they be matched to the letters on the table.

69. Materials needed:
1 set of capital letter cards (can use 1 set from game 60)

Directions for making:
See game 60; make only one set

Procedure:
Show your child the capital letter cards one at a time and ask the name of each letter. Name the letters your child does not know and help find the letter again in the yellow pages of your phone book.

70. Materials needed:
5 word cards

Directions for making:
Write one word in capital letters on each of five 3″ x 5″ cards. For example, cat, table, boy

Procedure:

Look at the word cards with your child, one at a time. Read the word aloud. Help your child name each letter. You might continue this game with other words, using letters with which your child has difficulty, as long as he or she is interested.

71. Materials needed:
    Several children's books
    Procedure:
    Using some of your child's own books ask that the letters in the titles be named.

*72. Materials needed:
    1 set of capital letter cards (as in game 60 or 68)
    Directions for making:
    See game 60
    Procedure:
    Show letters in random order one at a time. Ask your child to name each letter.

73. Materials needed:
    1 set large lowercase letters on 8½" x 11" paper

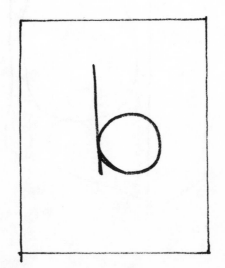

Directions for making:

On 8½″ x 11″ paper write one lowercase letter per sheet

Procedure:

Place the letter "a" in an obvious place in your home, perhaps taped to the front of the refrigerator. Tell your child the name of the letter and ask that he or she repeat the name. Refer to the letter often during the day asking each time for its name. Replace with a new letter every few days.

74. Materials needed:

A cereal box

Procedure:

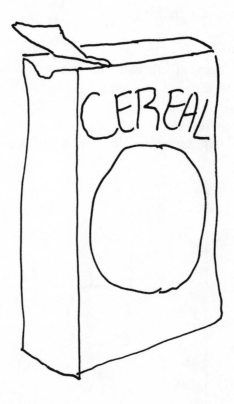

Point to different lowercase letters shown on the cereal box, one at a time and ask your child to name them. Name the ones missed and refer back to them after a few minutes to see if your child can remember their names.

75. Materials needed:
    A children's book
    Procedure:
    Choose a book that doesn't have too many words on each page. Play a game with your child. Say "I'm looking for a small letter 'b.' Can you find one?" Let your child show you a "b" on the page if he or she can. Then your child might name a letter for you to find. Continue with other letters on the page.

*76. Materials needed:
    1 set of lowercase letter cards (can use set from game 62)
    Directions for making:
    Follow directions in game 62
    Procedure:
    Show letters in random order one at a time. Ask your child to name each letter.

77. Materials needed:
    1 set of lowercase letter cards (can use set from game 62)
    Directions for making:
    See game 62
    Procedure:
    Show your child the lowercase letter cards one at a time. Help your child find the corresponding capital letter in a catalog or magazine.

78. Materials needed:
    1 set of lowercase letter cards (can use set from game 62)
    1 set folded capital/lowercase cards

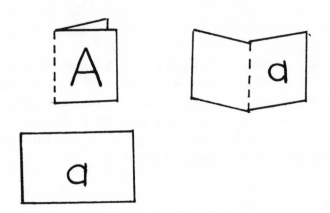

Directions for making:
    For directions for making a set of lowercase letter cards see game 62. To make folded capital/lowercase cards fold twenty-six 3″ x 5″ cards in half as shown. Write the capital letters, one per card, on the outside of each folded card. Open the card and write the corresponding lowercase letter inside.
Procedure:
    Place five or six folded cards on a table. Give the corresponding lowercase letter cards to your child and ask that he or she place each one with its corresponding capital. The card can then be opened to check and see if the choice was correct.

79. Materials needed:
    Capital/lowercase matching cards
    4 straws, pipe cleaners, sticks, or strips of paper

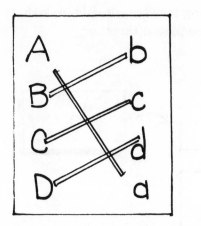 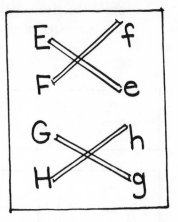

Directions for making:

On 8½″ x 11″ sheets of paper write four capital letters in a column on the left side and the corresponding lowercase letters out of order in a column on the right side. Continue with other cards and other letters.

Procedure:

Place one card at a time on a table. Give your child four items to connect the matching letters, such as straws, pipe cleaners, or strips of paper. Ask that your child lay each item across the sheet to connect the two letters that are the same.

*80. Materials needed:

1 set of capital letter cards (can use one set from game 60)

1 set lowercase letter cards (can use set from game 62)

Directions for making:

See directions for making capital letter cards in game 60

See directions for making lowercase letter cards in game 62

Procedure:

Place five capital letter cards on a table. Give your

child the five corresponding lowercase cards. Ask that
the corresponding cards be placed together.

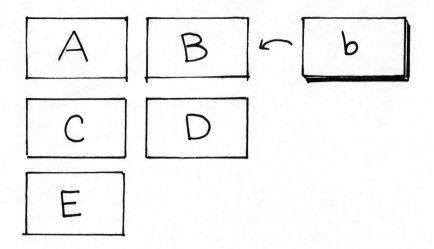

81. Materials needed:
    2 labels for familiar items in your child's room

Directions for making:
    On 3″ x 5″ cards print words to correspond with objects
    in your child's room, one word per card, such as door,
    toy, window, bed, lamp.
Procedure:
    Place a few labels in your child's room by taping the

cards to the correct items. Talk with your child about the word on each card. Add a new label everyday or so. You might later make another set of cards containing the same words and help your child find the two words that are exactly alike.

82. Materials needed:
     Pictures with words
     Matching word cards

Directions for making:
     On sixteen 3″ x 5″ cards draw or cut and glue sixteen

familiar pictures that have short words identifying
them, such as tree, cat, star, cake; one per card. Write
the correct word under each picture, also write the
matching words on separate cards; one per card.
Procedure:
Place four picture cards and four matching word cards
randomly on a table. Ask your child to put together the
word card with the correct picture card and tell you the
word that names the picture.

83. Materials needed:
    4 color cards
    4 color word cards

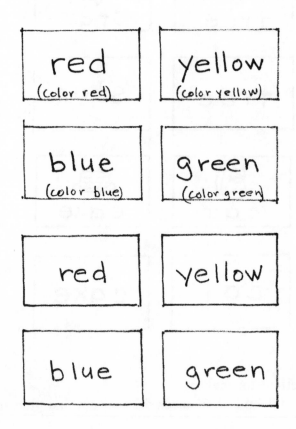

Directions for making:
On two 3″ x 5″ cards write the word red, on two write the word yellow, on two write the word blue, and on two green. With matching crayons color one card red that says red, color one yellow, one blue, and one green. Do not color the other four cards.

Procedure:
Place all eight cards randomly on a table. Ask your child to place together the words that are exactly alike. Ask your child the name of each color word. Give help if necessary.

*84. Materials needed:
2 sets of word cards

Directions for making:
On eight 3″ x 5″ cards write the following words, one per card: red, yellow, blue, green, cat, ball, dog, sun.

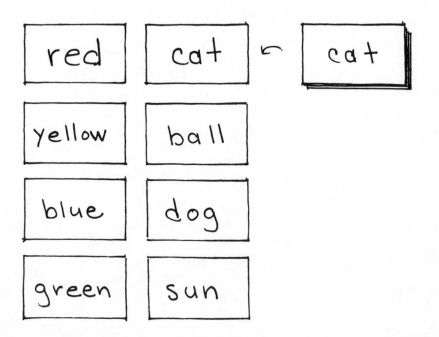

Repeat this procedure to make a second set of cards for matching.

Procedure:

Place one set of word cards on a table. Give the second set to your child and ask that they be matched to the cards on the table.

V.

Listening Games

1. Procedure:

   When people move they make many different kinds of sounds. As you walk across the room, you can hear footsteps. What does it sound like to walk down steps, to hop on one foot, to run down a sidewalk? Let your child experiment making different sounds by the way he or she moves. Then you might ask your child to try identifying some of the sounds you make while closing his or her eyes.

2. Procedure:

   Many things make sounds as they move. Cars make sounds, so do trucks, motorcycles, fire engines, buses, and airplanes. Can your child distinguish between such sounds? Help your child note these sounds while you are out walking so that an awareness of differences in sounds will be developed.

3. Procedure:

   Animals make different sounds. Name some animals for your child and ask what sounds each makes, such as dog, cat, cow, pig, horse, and so on. What other animals does your child know? You might like to choose a book on animals from the library to add additional learning. As your child learns the various sounds different animals make you might teach or sing together "Old MacDonald Had a Farm."

*4. Materials needed:

A door to open and close

A water faucet to turn on

A sheet of paper to tear

Procedure:

Tell your child that you will make some sounds that he or she has heard before. Ask your child to close his or her eyes. First open and close a door and ask what makes this sound. Then turn on a water faucet and ask what makes this sound. Finally, tear a sheet of paper and ask what sound this is.

5. Materials needed:

A radio

Procedure:

Listen to music on the radio. Turn the volume up and down. Talk about when it is loud and when it is soft. Have your child then tell you when it is loud and when soft.

6. Procedure:

Ask your child to sing an easy song that he or she knows such as "Twinkle, Twinkle, Little Star" or "Mary Had a Little Lamb." Ask that it first be sung as softly as possible and then be sung much louder.

7. Materials needed:

A small jar with lid

Several small objects such as a nail, a cotton ball, a few dried beans, a pencil eraser

Procedure:

Place each object in the jar one at a time, close the lid,

and shake. Listen to the sounds with your child and discuss them. Which sounds are soft? Which are loud?

*8. Materials needed:
A book
Procedure:
Tell your child to listen for a loud sound and a soft sound. Open the book and close it gently. Open the book and close it quickly. Repeat this asking your child each time if the sound was loud or soft.

9. Procedure:
Discuss with your child what sounds these animals make: baby chickens—peep, peep, peep. Are their sounds long or short? A growling bear—Gr-r-r-r-r. Long or short? Can your child imitate other animal's sounds that are long and some that are short?

10. Procedure:
Ask your child to walk across the room while humming. Then ask that he or she hum while only walking a few steps. Which hum was longer? You might suggest similar comparisons such as walking to a chair and to a door.

11. Procedure:
Ask your child if you beep a car horn once would the sound be long or short. What about a police siren blowing? Listen to sounds outside and talk about them with your child. Ask which are long and which are short. Perhaps you might hear the wind, a motorcycle or car passing, a lawn mower, the tapping of a woodpecker, or a car door slam. Your child might like to make different sounds outside and determine if they are long or short.

*12. Procedure:

Tell your child that you will hum a long sound and a short sound and to listen closely to each. First hum for about five seconds, then hum for about two seconds. Repeat the humming asking which sound is longer, which is shorter.

13. Procedure:

What objects in your home make noises? Perhaps you have a fan, an air conditioner, a washing machine, a clock, or a door bell. See how many things your child can find that make noises.

14. Materials needed:

A catalog

Procedure:

Cut out a number of pictures of objects that make sounds such as a dog, truck, clock, vacuum cleaner, typewriter. Show them one at a time and ask your child what sound each item makes.

15. Materials needed:

Small objects with which to make noise such as spoons, wooden or plastic blocks, a glass, a pencil, keys, etc.

Procedure:

Let your child experiment with sounds. Offer some items that can be tapped or used for tapping such as something metal, something wood, plastic, and perhaps glass. You might suggest gently tapping a glass with a metal spoon and a plastic spoon or tapping a glass and a plastic cup with a metal spoon. Does wood sound different from plastic when it is tapped? Which items make similar sounds?

*16. Materials needed:

3 containers—glasses, jars, or empty cans

    1 tablespoon uncooked rice
    1 nail
    3 buttons
Procedure:
    In one container place the rice, in another the nail, and in the third the buttons. Ask your child to shake each container gently and listen to the sounds. Then ask that your child's eyes be closed while you shake one. Can your child tell you which container you shook? Continue with the other two containers.

17. Procedure:
    Count from one to five beginning in a very low voice and ending on five in a high voice. Count backwards from five to one coming down the scale. Talk with your child about the sounds going up and down. Your child might like to try counting again with you.

18. Materials needed:
    A real or toy instrument, if available
Procedure:
    Using a piano, guitar, xylophone, or other instrument (real or toy) play the notes of the scale first up, then down. You may sing or hum the notes if you have no access to an instrument. Talk with your child about how the notes go up and down, which notes are called high and which are low.

19. Materials needed:
    3 empty boxes, different sizes
Procedure:
    Tap each box and listen with your child to the sound. Which sound is the highest and which is the lowest?

*20. Materials needed:

3 glasses containing varying amounts of water
1 metal spoon
Procedure:
Place the three glasses of water in a row on a table in order of the amount of water they contain. Let your child tap each with the spoon. Ask your child which sound is the highest? Which is the lowest?

21. Procedure:
Read nursery rhymes with your child and discuss which words rhyme because they sound similar. Help your child choose the words that rhyme in each poem.

22. Procedure:
Read familiar nursery rhymes leaving out the rhyming word. Ask your child to supply each correct word. For example:

> Little Miss Muffit
> Sat on a _____
> Eating her curds and whey.
> Along came a spider.
> And sat down beside _____
> And frightened Miss Muffit _____ .

Continue this with many familiar nursery rhymes and poems.

23. Procedure:
Read the following poem and see if your child can supply the correct words.

> We crept outside as quiet as could be
> And looked up above in the leaves of a _____ .
> Singing a lovely song we heard,
> Was a small brown feathered _____ .
> He saw us and he flew away,
> But we hoped he'd come another _____ .

*24. Materials needed:
 The following short poems:

> I walked across the floor
> To open the door.

> I had a little fish.
> He lived in a dish.

> I like to play and run.
> It's lots and lots of fun.

Procedure:
 Read each poem to your child one at a time. Ask which words rhyme. Give the following as an example.

> The pillow is red,
> That lies on my bed.

Explain that "red" and "bed" rhyme because they sound very much alike.

25. Materials needed:
 Pairs of objects with names that rhyme such as

> rope and soap
> rock and block
> mop and top
> fan and pan

Any other combinations of objects whose names rhyme would be suitable.
Procedure:
 Choose two pairs of objects at a time with which to work, such as a rope, soap, rock, and block. Place all four objects on a table. With your child talk about each object and ask "What is its name?" Help your child to group together each pair of objects with names that

rhyme. Try to think of other combinations of objects you have in your home, as the more experiences you give your child the easier it will be to learn rhyming sounds.

26. Materials needed:
    Several household objects with one-syllable names such as book, door, spoon, rug.
    Procedure:
    Show one object at a time to your child and ask its name. Then ask if there is another word that rhymes with its name. If you show a book, your child might say cook, look, or hook for example. Give help if necessary. See how many rhyming words you can think of together. Continue with other objects as long as your child shows an interest.

27. Materials needed:
    Items listed in game 25 or similar items
    A paper sack
    Procedure:
    Using pairs of objects that you have already used in game 25, one pair at a time, place one object of the pair in a paper bag and the other object on a table. For example place the rope in a bag and the soap on a table. Ask your child to feel the soap and tell you what it is. Then ask your child to reach into the bag without looking, feel the object, and tell you what it is that rhymes with soap. Continue with other pairs. If you did not do game 25 previously, it would be helpful to look at and name all the objects you will be using before beginning. If you are using objects that are too large to fit in a paper sack, you might have your child close his or her eyes when the object is being felt.

*28. Materials needed:

GROUP 1

A piece of string
A ring
A book

GROUP 2

A pair of socks
A box
A comb

GROUP 3

A glass
A piece of grass
A spoon

Procedure:
Place one group of three objects at a time on a table.
Ask your child to name each object in the group and
choose two objects that rhyme. Do the same with the
other two groups.

29. Materials needed:
Comic strip from the newspaper
Procedure:
Read a familiar comic strip to your child. Talk about
what you see in the pictures. Name a word that rhymes
with an object pictured and see if your child can find
the objects. For example you might say "bee" if there
were a "tree" pictured. Give hints and help if necessary.

30. Materials needed:
    A picture book
    Procedure:
    Look at a picture book with your child. Say a word that
    rhymes with something pictured on each page if possi-
    ble. Ask your child to find the item that rhymes with
    the word you give. Give other clues to finding the
    rhyming picture if necessary.

31. Materials needed:
    8½″ x 11″ paper
    Crayons
    Procedure:
    Ask your child to draw a picture of the following items,
    one per page: dog, sun, pie. You might write the name
    of each item under the picture. Place the three pictures
    on a table before your child. Tell your child you will
    say some words and ask that he or she choose the pic-
    ture that rhymes with each word each time. Say the
    following words in this order one at a time giving time
    for your child to choose the right picture: run, fly, log,
    fun, frog, cry. Help your child if necessary.

*32. Materials needed:
    Pictures of a book, chair, bat, coat, fan, clock
    Directions for making:
    On 3″ x 5″ cards draw or cut and glue pictures of a book,
    a chair, a bat, a coat, a fan, and a clock, one per card.
    Procedure:
    Place all cards on a table. Say the following words one
    at a time, and ask your child to point to the picture
    whose name rhymes with each word: cook, rock, goat,
    man, bear, and hat.

33. Materials needed:
    Rhyme puzzles
    Directions for making:
    Make a rhyme puzzle by drawing or cutting and gluing
    two pictures with names that rhyme on a 3″ x 5″ card.
    Cut, puzzle fashion, between the pictures. Make a
    number of these puzzles cutting each differently.

Procedure:
Place on a table three rhyme puzzles at a time with their pieces separated and randomly placed. Ask your child to first name each picture, then put the rhyming pictures together to complete the puzzles.

34. Materials needed:
Pictures of the following: a swing, a ring, a flower, a hook, a book, a flag, a car, a star, and an apple.

Directions for making:
Draw or cut and glue pictures of the following items on
3″ x 5″ cards: swing, ring, flower, hook, book, flag, car,
star, and apple.
Procedure:
Place unmatched on a table three pictures at a time,
two that rhyme and one that doesn't. For example: a
swing, a ring, and a flower. Ask your child to name
each picture and put together the two pictures whose
name rhyme.

35. Materials needed:
Rhyming lotto game
2 playing cards
8 matching cards

Pictures for Playing Cards

1.	Box	5.	Frog
2.	Bread	6.	Moon
3.	Bug	7.	Duck
4.	Skate	8.	Can

Pictures for Matching Cards

1.	Socks	5.	Log
2.	Bed	6.	Spoon
3.	Rug	7.	Truck
4.	Plate	8.	Man

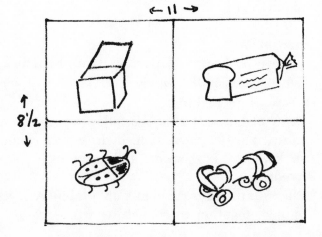

Directions for making:

You should make two playing cards. To make each, score an 8½″ x 11″ sheet of paper into four sections as shown. On each section draw or cut and glue one picture from the pictures for playing cards list. On eight 3″ x 5″ cards draw or cut and glue the pictures listed for matching cards, one per card.

Procedure:

Two players are needed; you may be the second player. Each player should have a card on a table. Place matching cards face down in a box. Each player takes a turn drawing a card from the box. If the name of the picture on the card drawn rhymes with the picture on the playing card of the one who draws, the drawn card is placed on the playing card. If it does not rhyme, it is returned to the box and the other player has a turn. The object is to match all the pictures with a rhyming picture card.

*36. Materials needed:

Picture cards of the following items; fish, dish, mouse, house, cake, snake, light, kite, spoon, and moon.

Directions for making:

Draw or cut and glue the following items on 3″ x 5″ cards, one per card: fish, dish, mouse, house, cake, snake, light, kite, spoon, and moon.

Procedure:

Place all pictures randomly on a table. Ask your child to place together those pictures whose names rhyme.

37. Procedure:

Play a rhyming word game with your child. Say, "I'm thinking of a word that rhymes with <u>boy</u>." Give appropriate hints if necessary such as "It's something to play with" or "you keep them on a shelf in your room." Use as many different words as you can think of for which your child can guess rhyming words.

38. Procedure:

Make a book of rhyming words. At the top of each page write one word such as cat. Your child might like to illustrate the picture. At the bottom of the page write all the words your child can think of that rhyme with cat such as bat, hat, rat, sat. Staple the pages into a book as you work with more words. At later dates you might like to review the book occasionally to see if your child can add additional words to it.

39. Procedure:

Help your child make up some two-line poems of his or her own. You might supply the first line and help your child think of the second line. These should be short and easy poems such as:

> We helped to clean the room.
> We used a mop and broom.

*40. Materials needed:

Picture cards of a bee, chair, can, and dog

Directions for making:

Draw or cut and glue a picture of a bee, a chair, a can, and a dog on 3″ x 5″ cards, one per card.

Procedure:
   Show the pictures to your child, one at a time. First ask your child to name the picture then tell you a word that rhymes with it.

41. Materials needed:
   A pen
   A picture
   A box
   A book
   A towel
   A top
   A nickel
   A nail

Procedure:
   Place all the items on a table. Ask your child to name each item. Group the items into pairs that begin with the same letter sound. Ask your child to again name the items in the pairs, this time listening to the beginning sounds. Help your child to hear the sounds that are alike. You might use other items that you have. (Avoid words beginning with vowels—a, e, i, o, and u—and the consonants c and g because their sounds vary too greatly.)

42. Procedure:
   Name an object found in your home such as a watch. Help your child listen to the beginning sound. Show your child another object beginning with that sound such as a window. Can he or she hear the same beginning sound? Continue with other beginning sounds of objects you might have such as letter and light, pan and pencil, and so on.

43. Procedure:

Talk about the sound at the beginning of your child's name. (If your child's name begins with a vowel or the consonants c or g, you might choose someone else's name.) Name other words that begin with the same sound as your child's name. Let your child repeat them to you. You might try this with other names. Perhaps your child would add some names that begin with the same sound as the names given.

*44. Materials needed:
One each of the following objects:
Box, book, pencil
Pen, picture, bottle
Ring, rock, glass
Towel, top, spoon
Nickel, nail, crayon
Procedure:
Place on a table the above five groups of objects, one group at a time. Ask your child to name each object in the group. Then ask which two objects begin with the same sound.

45. Materials needed:
A magazine picture
Procedure:
Choose a magazine picture that has several items in it. First ask your child to name the items in the picture. Name a word that has the same beginning sound as an item pictured. For example if your picture shows a table, you might say "toy." See if your child can find the pictured item that begins with the same sound as your word.

46. Procedure:
Cut out three pictures of items that begin with differ-

ent consonant sounds other than the consonants c and g. Let your child look at and name each picture. With your child look through a catalog or magazine and find another picture to represent each beginning sound. For example if you have pictures of a boy, a hat, and a lamp, you might find a bat, a house, and a ladder. Let your child cut out these pictures and help him or her hear the beginning sounds. Save all the pictures for game 47.

47. Materials needed:
    Pictures from game 46 and other similar picture pairs
    Procedure:
    With your child make a booklet of words that begin with the same sound. Help your child to group into pairs the pictures that begin alike. You and your child might like to add more picture pairs to represent other sounds (except for the vowels and consonants c and g). These can be worked on, a few at a time, over several weeks. Let your child glue each two pictures that begin alike on a separate sheet of 8½" x 11" paper. These can be stapled into a booklet and saved for later use.

*48. Materials needed:
    Picture cards of a ball, beads, sun, scissors, rug, and a ring.
    Directions for making:
    Draw or cut and glue pictures of a ball, beads, sun, scissors, rug, and a ring on separate 3" x 5" cards.

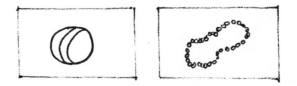

Procedure:

Place all cards unmatched on a table. Ask your child to place together those pictures with names beginning with the same sound.

49. Materials needed:

    Letter-picture puzzles

    Directions for making:

    On the right side of 3″ x 5″ cards draw or cut and glue pictures to represent different consonant sounds, other than the consonants c and g. Use one picture per card. Write the letter each picture begins with on the left side of each card. Cut each card into two pieces, puzzle

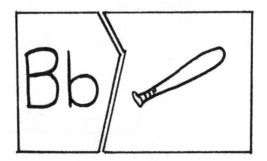

fashion, making each puzzle different. You might like to make a large assortment of these to help your child learn beginning sounds.

Procedure:

Place three puzzles at a time, separated and un-matched, on a table. Ask your child to put the puzzles together, to name each letter, and to name each picture.

50. Materials needed:

Pantry items such as cans and boxes of food

Procedure:

Look with your child at the labels on some of your cans or boxes of food. Help find the word on the label that names its contents. Help your child find the beginning letter, name it, and say the word. Listen to the sound it makes. Are these several items that begin with the same letter and same sound such as peas and peaches, mayonnaise and macaroni?

51. Materials needed:

A set of consonant letter cards (omit letters c and g)

Directions for making:

Using nineteen 3" x 5" cards write each consonant let-

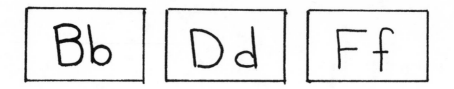

ter other than c and g in both its upper- and lowercase form on a separate card.

Procedure:

Show your child one letter card at a time. Name the letter and a word that begins with that letter. Help your child find an object in your home that starts with the same sound. For example you might show a Kk, say "kite," and help your child find a key. Continue with other letters as long as there is an interest.

*52. Materials needed:

Picture cards of a bell, hat, rug, tree, dog, and pan

Letter cards—Bb, Rr, and Pp (can use cards from game 51)

Directions for making:

See directions in game 51 for letter cards. Draw or cut out and glue on six 3″ x 5″ cards the pictures of a bell, hat, rug, tree, dog, and pan, one per card.

Procedure:

Place three cards on a table one group at a time (Bb, bell, and hat; Rr, rug, and tree; Pp, dog, and pan). Ask your child to name the letter and pictures, then choose the picture that begins with the sound of the letters shown. Do the same with the next two groups.

53. Materials needed:

Set of consonant letter cards omitting consonants c and g (can use cards from game 51).

Directions for making:

See game 51

Procedure:

Using the consonant letter cards show them one at a time to your child. Ask what the name of the letter is. Then help your child think of some words that begin with the sound each letter makes.

54. Materials needed:

Booklet from game 47.

Directions for making:

Make by directions given for game 47 if not already made.

Procedure:

Go through the booklet with your child asking which letter sound each page of pictures represents. Give assistance when necessary. You or your child can write the correct letter at the bottom of each page in both its capital and lowercase forms.

55. Materials needed:

Magazine or catalog

Procedure:

Look at pictures in a magazine or catalog with your child. Ask your child to name some of the items shown and try to tell you what letter sound begins each picture's name. Give help if necessary.

*56. Materials needed:

Letter cards Nn, Bb, and Pp (can use those from game 51)

Picture cards of a nut, banana, pencil, nest, balloon, and purse.

Directions for making:

See game 51 for directions for letter cards. Draw or cut and glue pictures of a nut, banana, pencil, nest, balloon, and purse on six 3″ x 5″ cards, one per card.

Procedure:

Place the three letter cards in a row across a table. Give the picture to your child one at a time and ask that each be placed under the letter which begins the word naming the picture.

Appendices

A.

Book List

Hardcover editions of the books listed here are still in print. Those preceded by an asterisk are also available in paperback.

Aardema, Verna. *Why Mosquitoes Buzz in People's Ears: A West African Tale.* New York: Dial, 1975.

Anderson, Ann. *The Old Mother Goose.* New York: Thomas Nelson, 1925.

Ardizzone, Aingelda. *The Night Ride.* New York: Windmill/Dutton, 1975.

Asch, Frank. *Good Lemonade.* New York: Watts, 1976.

Bailey, Carolyn. *The Little Rabbit That Wished for Red Wings.* New York: Platt and Munk, 1945.

Bate, Norman. *Who Built the Bridge?* New York: Scribner, 1954.

*Bemelmans, Ludwig. *Madeline.* New York: Viking Press, 1939.

Berson, Harold. *I'm Bored, Ma!* New York: Crown, 1976.

Beskow, Elsa. *Pelle's New Suit.* New York: Harper, 1929.

Bragg, Mabel, retold by Watty Paper. *The Little Engine That Could.* New York: Platt and Munk, 1930.

Brown, Marcia. *Once a Mouse.* New York: Scribner, 1961.

*_____.. *Three Billy Goats Gruff*. New York: Harcourt, Brace, 1957.

*Brown, Margaret Wise. *The Country Noisy Book*. New York: Harper, 1940.

*_____. *The Golden Egg Book*. New York: Golden Press, 1976.

Burningham, John. *Mr. Grumpy's Motor Car*. New York: Crowell, 1976.

*Burton, Virginia L. *Katy and the Big Snow*. Boston: Houghton Mifflin, 1943.

_____. *The Little House*. Boston: Houghton Mifflin, 1942.

_____. *Mike Mulligan and His Steam Shovel*. Boston: Houghton Mifflin, 1939.

Conford, Ellen. *Just the Thing for Geraldine*. Boston: Little, Brown, 1974.

Conover, Chris. *Six Little Ducks*. New York: Crowell, 1976.

*Davis, Alice Vaught. *Timothy Turtle*. New York: Harcourt, Brace, 1940.

de Angeli, Marguerite. *Book of Nursery and Mother Goose Rhymes*. New York: Doubleday, 1954.

Delafield, Celia. *Mrs. Mallard's Ducklings*. New York: Lothrop, Lee and Shepard, 1946.

*De Regniers, Beatrice Schenk. *May I Bring a Friend?* New York: Atheneum, 1964.

*Emberley, Barbara. *Drummer Hoff*. Englewood Cliffs: Prentice-Hall, 1967.

Flack, Marjorie. *Angus and the Cat*. New York: Doubleday, 1931.

*_____. *Angus and the Ducks*. New York: Doubleday, 1930.

_____. *The Restless Robin*. Boston: Houghton Mifflin, 1937.

*_____. *The Story About Ping*. New York: Viking Press, 1933.

_____. *Tim Tadpole and the Great Bullfrog*. New York: Doubleday, 1959.

_____. *Wait for William*. Boston: Houghton Mifflin, 1935.

Gag, Wanda. *ABC Bunny*. New York: Coward-McCann, 1933.

———. *Millions of Cats*. New York: Coward-McCann, 1935.

Gramatky, Hardy. *Little Toot*. New York: G. P. Putnam, 1939.

*Hader, Berta, and Elmer Hader. *The Big Snow*. New York: Macmillan, 1948.

*Haley, Gail E. *A Story—A Story*. New York: Atheneum, 1970.

Hall, Adelaide. *The Parade*. New York: Watts, 1975.

*Heyward, Dubose, and Majorie Flack. *Country Bunny and the Little Gold Shoes*. Boston: Houghton Mifflin, 1939.

Hoban, Russell C. *Ten What?* New York: Scribner, 1975.

*Hogrogian, Nonny. *One Fine Day*. New York: Macmillan, 1971.

Keats, Ezra Jack. *Snowy Day*. New York: Viking Press, 1962.

*Langstaff, John. *Frog Went A-Courtin'*. New York, Harcourt, 1955.

Lindman, Maj. *Snipp, Snapp, Snurr and the Red Shoes*. Chicago: Albert Whitman, 1932.

*Lipkind, Will. *Finders Keepers*. New York: Harcourt, Brace, 1951.

*McCloskey, Robert. *Blueberries for Sal*. New York: Viking Press, 1948.

*———. *Make Way for Ducklings*. New York: Viking Press, 1941.

McDermott, Gerald. *Arrow to the Sun*. New York: Viking Press, 1974.

Mayer, Mevcer. *AH-CHOO*. New York: Dial, 1976.

Milhous, Katherine. *The Egg Tree*. New York: Scribner, 1950.

Moore, Clement. *The Night Before Christmas*. New York: Houghton Mifflin, 1958.

Mosel, Arlene. *The Funny Little Woman*. New York: Dutton, 1972.

Ness, Evaline. *Sam, Bangs and Moonshine*. New York: Holt, 1966.

Newberry, Clare. *April's Kitten*. New York: Harper, 1940.

————. *Mittens*. New York: Harper, 1936.

*Nic Leodhas, Sohche. *Always Room For One More*. New York: Holt, 1965.

*Payne, Emmy. *Katy-No-Pocket*. Boston: Houghton Mifflin, 1944.

Perrault, Charles, retold by. *Cinderella*. New York: Henry Z. Walck, 1971.

Ranson, Arthur. *The Fool of the World and the Flying Ship*. New York: Farrar, Straus, 1968.

*Rey, H. A. *Curious George*. Boston: Houghton Mifflin, 1941.

————. *Curious George Gets a Medal*. Boston: Houghton Mifflin, 1957.

Rice, Eve. *Oh Lewis!* New York: Macmillan, 1974.

Robbins, Ruth. *Baboushka and the Three Kings*. Berkeley: Parnassus, 1960.

Rose, Anne. *As Right As Right Can Be*. New York: Dial, 1976

Sendak, Maurice. *Where the Wild Things Are*. New York: Harper, 1963.

Seuss, Dr. *And to Think That I Saw It on Mulberry Street*. New York: Vanguard Press, 1937.

————. *Cat in the Hat*. New York: Random House, 1957.

————. *Green Eggs and Ham*. New York: Random House, 1960.

Simon, Norma. *All Kinds of Families*. Chicago: Whitman, 1975.

*Slobodkina, Esphyr. *Caps for Sale*. New York: William R. Scott, 1947.

*Steig, William. *Sylvester and the Magic Pebble*. New York: Windmill Books/Simon and Schuster, 1969.

*Thurber, James. *Many Moons*. New York: Harcourt, Brace, 1943.

Tresselt, Alvin. *Autumn Harvest*. New York: Lothrop, Lee and Shepard, 1951.

_____. *Hi! Mr. Robin!* New York: Lothrop, Lee and Shepard, 1950.

_____. *Rain Drop Splash*. New York: Lothrop, Lee and Shepard, 1946.

Tudor, Tasha. *Mother Goose*. New York: Henry Z. Walck, 1957.

Waber, Bernard. *But Names Will Never Hurt Me*. Boston: Houghton Mifflin, 1976.

Yashima, Taro. *Crow Boy*. New York: Viking Press, 1955.

Zemach, Harve. *Duffy and the Devil*. New York: Farrar, Straus & Giroux, 1973.

Zolotow, Charlotte. *The Summer Night*. New York: Harper, 1974.

Record List

INTERPRETATIVE RHYTHMS

Animals and Toys, Evans, Ruth—Evans Record Company
> Duck, Camels, Horses, Elephants, Trains, Tops, Soldiers, Airplanes

Circus, Wood, Lucille, and Ruth Turner—Bowmar
> Circus Parade; Merry-Go-Round; Circus Ponies (Gallop and High Step and Trot); Trapeze Performers (Swing, Clown, Shuffle); Walk, Run, and Fall; Elephants; Lions, Monkeys

Farm Animals, James, Phoebe—Phoebe James Rhythms Record Company
> Cows, Ducks, Chickens, etc.

My Playful Scarf—Children's Record Guild

MUSIC FOR QUIET LISTENING

Basic Christmas Album—Victor
1. Under the Stars, Davis-Brown; I Saw Three Ships, English Traditional Melody; Once in Royal David's City,

Alexander-Gauntlett; Jingle Bells, Pierpoint; Away in the Manger, Luther; I Heard the Bells on Christmas Day, Gilchrist.

2. While Shepherds Watched Their Flocks by Night, Handel; Joy to the World, Handel; It Came Upon the Midnight Clear, Willis; The First Nowell, Old Carol; Deck the Halls with Boughs of Holly, Old Welsh Air

Basic Listening Program—Nos. 1, 2, Vol. I—Victor
1. Lullaby, Brahms; Little Sandman, Brahms; Hush My Babe, Rousseau; Lullaby, Mozart; Cradle Song, Schubert; Sweet and Low, Barnby

2. March of the Little Lead Soldiers. Pierné; Petite Suite, (a) March (Trumpet and Drums), (b) Impromptu (The Top). Bizet

Basic Listening Program—Nos. 1, 4, Vol. III—Victor
1. Marionettes, "Woodland Sketches." (a) Witch, (b) Clown, (c) Villian, MacDowell: Ol' Br'er Rabbit. MacDowell: To a Water Lily, MacDowell

2. The Bee, Schubert; Waltz in D Flat, Chopin; Spring Song, Mendelssohn

Child's Introduction to Folk Music—Wonderland Records

In a Clock Store—Victor Concert Orchestra—Victor

MUSIC FOR STUDIED LISTENING

March of the Toys, Herbert—Decca Album DA 419

Rhythm Orchestra, James, Phoebe—Phoebe James Rhythms
Record Company
    Indians (Drums), Clocks (Tone Blocks), Woodpeckers
    (Rhythm Sticks), Rain (Maracas), In Mexico (Tam-
    bourines), Jingle Bells (Bells)

Music Differentiating Pitch—High and Low
Csarda (Xylophone)—Decca
Drummer Boy—Young People's Records
Witch, The, Tchaikovsky—Basic Rhythms Program Vol.
III—Victor

Music Differentiating Intensity—Loud and Soft
Hungarian Rhapsody, Adler—Decca
Lullaby, Brahms—Basic Listening Program Vol. I—Victor
March of the Little Lead Soldiers, Pierné—Basic Listening
    Program Vol. I—Victor

Music Differentiating Tempo—Fast and Slow
Badinage, Herbert—Basic Listening Program Vol. I—Victor
Hungarian Dances, Brahms—Decca Album

Music Differentiating Phrasing and Recurring Theme
Hungarian Folk Song Fantasy—Decca

Ensemble Effects and Individual Instruments
A Child's Introduction to the Musical Instruments—Golden
    Records
Little Fiddle, with Danny Kaye—Decca
Meet the Instruments of the Orchestra (one LP recording and
    two full-color filmstrips)—Bowmar; Strings, Wood-
    winds, Brass, and Percussion
Peter and the Wolf (simplified), Boris Karloff, narrator—
    Mercury Records
Tubby the Tuba, Victor Jory, narrator—Columbia Records

Alphabet

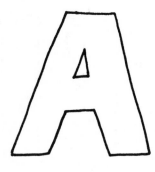 

 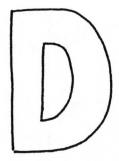

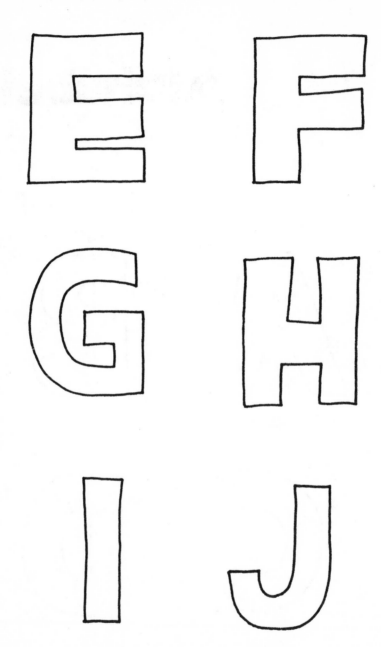

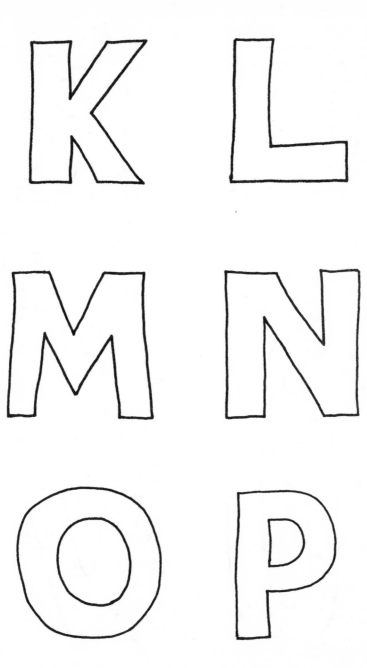

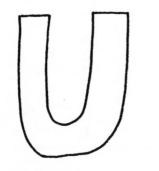

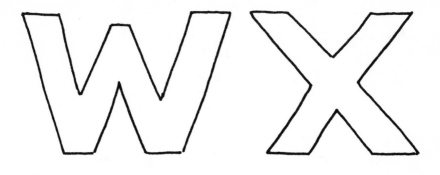

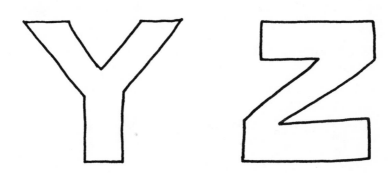

Index